I WANT TO BE A
PHYSIOTHERAPIST

Written by
Jonathan Reule

Illustration
Caballero Peza Mauricio
&
Caballero Peza Gabriel Fernando

Storyboard
Shermaine See

First paperback edition May 2023
ISBN 978-981-18-6794-1

Published by Unibino Pte. Ltd.
31 Rochester Drive Level 3, #03-47 Singapore 138637

www.unibino.com

Have you ever had an injury that stopped you from doing the things you love? Maybe you sprained your ankle playing soccer or broke your arm falling off your bike. It can be tough to recover from these injuries and get back to normal. And for even bigger injuries, it could take even longer to resume your normal life.
HOSPITAL

This is why physiotherapists are so important in our modern world. They're experts who know how to help people recover from injuries and build up strength. They work with all kinds of patients, from athletes to children who need help with their physical development, and sometimes people who just want to feel better. So if you like helping people build up their physical strength and have a lot of patience, then being a physiotherapist could be a great career for you!

Before we delve deeper into this profession, let's take a moment to understand how it came to be and why it remains crucial in our modern-day world. It all started with our early ancestors. Although humans have always been tough and resilient, our bodies are still vulnerable vessels.

In ancient times we used to be more active than we are today, which kept our bodies fit and in shape. But unfortunately, that didn't protect us from the many dangers around us. There were wild animals ready to attack us, falling trees during thunderstorms, steep drops from mountainsides, and illnesses that could strike us at any moment!

These are of course still dangers in our modern world, but in ancient times we didn't have the medical advancements that we have today to help us if we were to get into such an accident. If a person were to hurt their legs badly enough, they might get left behind by others instead of being given the care they need to rehabilitate.

The other problem was the ancient's lack of knowledge pertaining to our physical bodies. Even if a person wasn't left behind after sustaining an injury, the kind individuals around them might not know the best way to help their bodies heal, which could lead to bad advice and potentially worsen their condition!

But as time progressed and civilisations started to bloom around the world, we not only had more resources and larger cities but also new specialised professions that could make our lives easier. Doctors, healers, and medical practitioners were some of those early professions that came along with the advances in civilisation.

This allowed people to focus on one area of study and learn as much as they could over their lifetimes, then give back that knowledge to others. Hippocrates is one such example. He spent much of his time studying human anatomy and physiology and is considered by many to be the very first recorded practitioner of physiotherapy! Hippocrates realised that massages and warm water therapies were great treatments for people who'd sustained debilitating injuries. In fact, he often prescribed these treatments to his patients, who showed a better rate of recovery than without these remedies.

Despite the fact that there isn't much information on physiotherapy after these instances in our history, there are other examples of physical therapies, such as massages and hydro therapies. For instance, the Japanese have documents from as far back as the 6th century, listing the benefits of relaxing in hot springs to help with muscle pains and joint ailments.

What's even more interesting is that the Japanese used these hot springs as a place for therapy by doing specific movements in the warm water to ease discomfort or to help strengthen their bodies. They also had a reputation for massages that focused on specific pressure points to heal the body. This technique later came to be known as Shiatsu massages.

It wasn't until the early 1800s that physiotherapy was considered a formal profession on its own accord. It began in Sweden with a doctor named Pehr Henrik Ling, who used therapeutic techniques on gymnasts after their rigorous training and intense performances.

Then by the end of the century, physiotherapy became officially recognised as a profession in all of Sweden and soon extended to other places in the world.

In the US, Physiotherapy came to be established as a vitally important profession during the 1900s, when doctors began paying more attention to children born with physical disabilities, especially during the polio pandemic. This is where many of their experimental exercises and treatments were first put into practice, in a hospital-like setting.

In no time, physical therapists became a standard profession in most hospitals worldwide. As medical sciences started to advance and more research was done within the field, people began to recognise the great benefits offered by physical therapy, not only for people with pain and disabilities but also individuals recovering from surgeries.

But this may have you wondering what exactly physiotherapists do. Why are they important in our modern world, and how can you become one yourself? Physical therapists have a wide range of functions and responsibilities - from helping sports players with pain management to working with individuals to regain their mobility after strokes and other neurological diseases, but of course, that's not all.

For starters, being a physiotherapist requires patience and discipline when helping clients, as most will try to achieve small manageable goals each session. This job also demands that you stay fit and keep up your health to offer your clients the best level of care. Another key quality is to have good communication skills, as physical therapists should be able to explain the exercises to their patients clearly and concisely.

Physiotherapists should also be good at managing several clients within a day. This means they need to be punctual and stick to their scheduled exercises in order to have enough time for all their patients. Lastly, physiotherapists should be well-trained and educated in their field while keeping up to date on the newest findings and practices available.

On a daily basis, a physiotherapist may be busy with an assortment of tasks. They may be working with new clients, assessing their capabilities and making a program according to their needs. They may also find themselves updating spreadsheets to help them keep track of their regular clients, to make sure the program is working, and to decide if they need to increase the challenges.

Physiotherapists also need to make sure that their equipment is well-maintained and ready to use every day. Physical therapists sometimes will use warm tubs for hydrotherapy, TENS machines for electrotherapy, and other devices such as resistance bands needed for rehabilitation. And if they don't maintain these items properly, then they won't be able to help their clients to the best of their abilities.

Now you may be asking what does it take to become a qualified physiotherapist? Most have their bachelor's degrees in physical therapy or a similar field of study. Some physiotherapists also apply for a degree apprenticeship where they can study while practising under a mentor's guidance.
PHYSIOTHERAPY
MEDICAL BOOK
ANATOMY

After this, physical therapists can go on to get a postgraduate degree, either to specialise in one specific field of physiotherapy or to better their chances of landing a job once they graduate. From that point onward, though, you'll need to find a clinic or hospital looking for new physiotherapists to join their teams so that you can get plenty of practical experience working on the job.

PEDIATRIC   --
NEURO   P.23
MUSCOKETAL   P.24
SPORTS   P.25
VESTIVULAR   P.26
ORTHOPEDIC   P.27
Next, you'll want to decide what type of physical therapist you'd like to be. There are several different options within this field, each with its own focus and methods for rehabilitation. So you might also make your decision based on the type of clients you'd most likely enjoy working with!

Pediatric physiotherapists work with children from birth up into adolescence. These therapists are specially trained to work with children and can take into account their progress as they grow and mature. These physiotherapists also help children born with physical disabilities to help build up their strength or to increase their mobility as they age.

Neuro physiotherapists work with patients who've experienced neurological conditions that have also impacted their physical bodies. They may help individuals who've suffered from strokes, spinal cord injuries, or Parkinson's disease. These physiotherapists will need to be able to build individualised treatment plans for each of their clients.

Musculoskeletal physiotherapists deal with the muscular and skeletal systems, working with patients to either recuperate after a surgery or injury or to help alleviate pain from those areas. This could require the therapists to know several different techniques, from acupuncture to deep tissue massages and even electrotherapy in some cases.

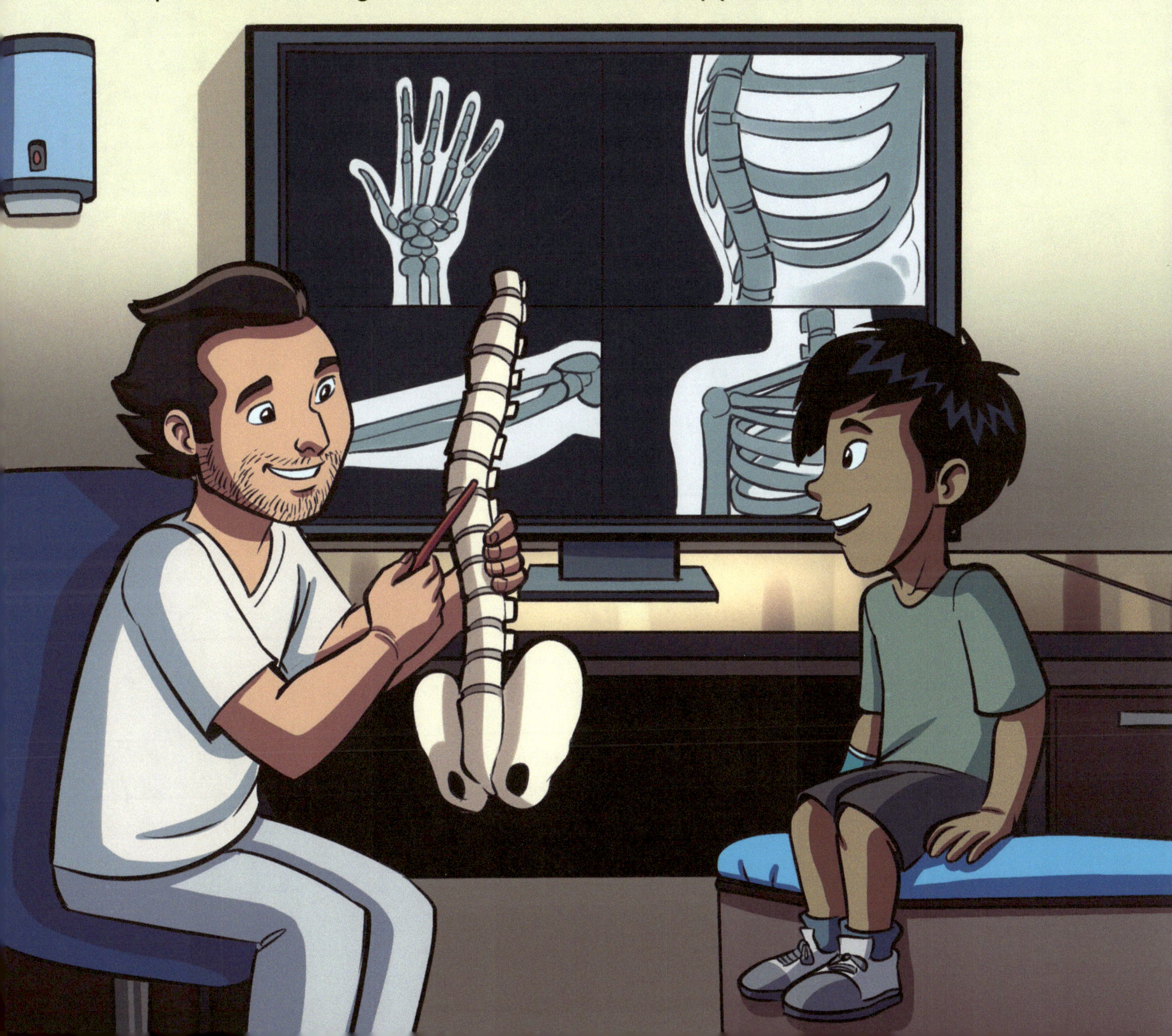

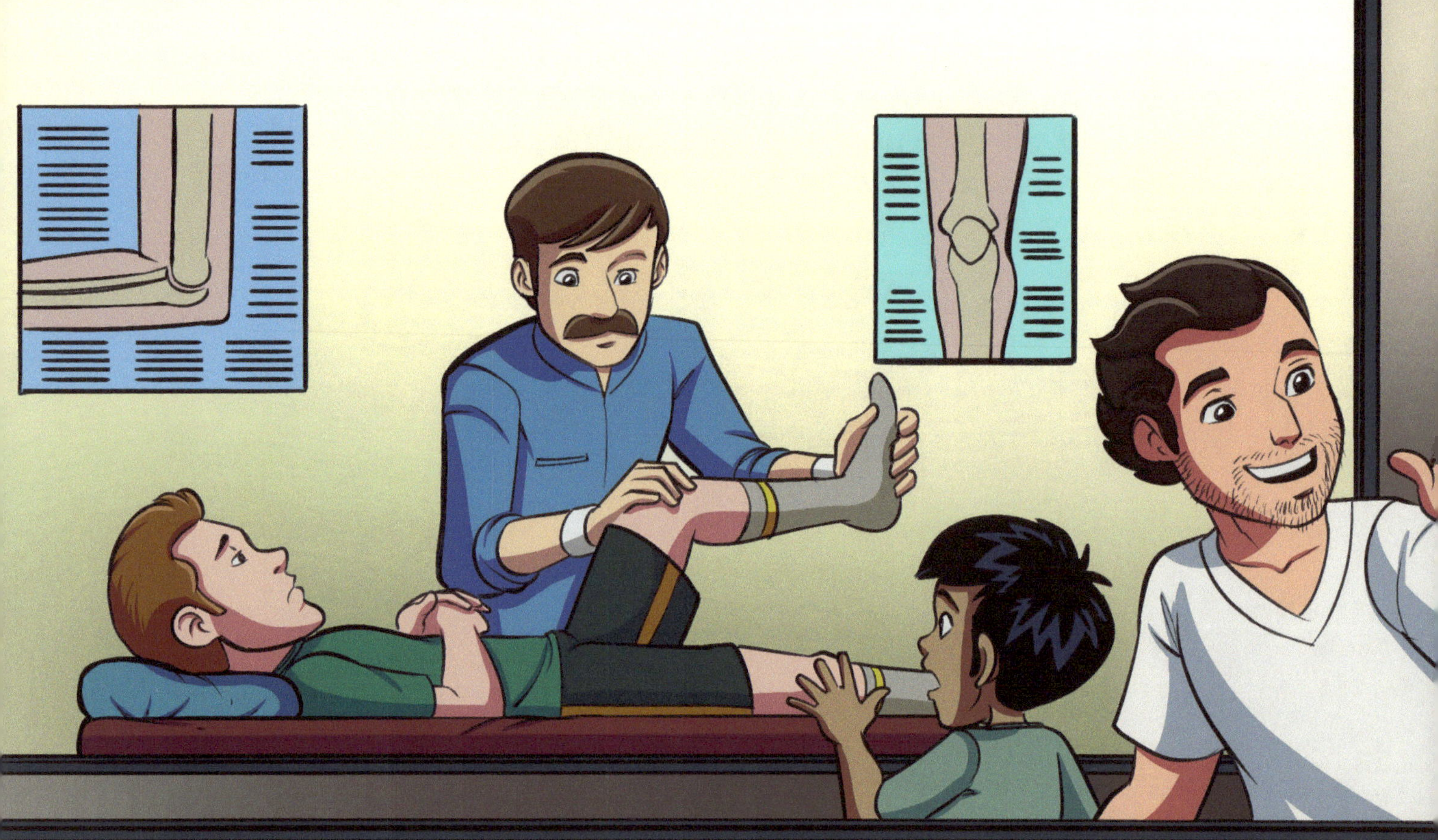

Sports physiotherapists also deal with joint pains and muscle tensions, but they're different in that they work primarily with athletes. They may tag along with the professional athletes as they go from location to location, ensuring they are well taken care of while performing on the field. Sports physiotherapists also help with specific injuries or strains caused by repetitive actions, which are common in most sports. Think about a golfer who has to swing their clubs in the same motion every day.

Vestibular physiotherapists help their clients manage vertigo or other balance-related issues.

As the vestibular system inside the ear is the control centre of our balance, these physiotherapists often focus on helping patients to recalibrate their sense of balance by doing various exercises, such as eye movements or head movements, while trying to remain steady. People who have recently lost a limb, like a leg, or people who've experienced severe strokes usually need to consult with Vestibular Physiotherapists to help them with balance and dizziness issues.

Hand physiotherapy is a newer branch that pays attention to common pains and ailments that occur within the hand.
This may include patients suffering from arthritis, trigger fingers, congenital deformities, wrist dislocations, and injuries to the tendons or bones. For these physiotherapists, their treatments can take on a wide range of practices, depending on the severity of the client's problems.

Foot physiotherapists are similar, except that they focus on the client's feet and their associated problems. They can assist with issues ranging from the toes all the way back to the back heel. These physiotherapists typically identify the problem areas in the feet and create treatments to work with patients in those affected areas. This could be done by prescribing proper footwear, foot massages, or even exercises to rebuild weakened muscles and tendons.

In conclusion, with the advancements in medical science and technology, physiotherapy has become an integral part of modern healthcare. It has allowed individuals to regain their mobility, manage pain, and improve their overall quality of life.

But it's up to you whether you think this might be the right career to pursue. No matter what you may choose though, remember that with every job comes its own set of challenges and concerns.
It's important to keep in mind every day why you started and how your work benefits the many patients in need of physical therapy in our modern world.

Shubhi Saxena
Founder, Unibino

My Inspiration

As a parent in this ever-changing world, it can sometimes feel overwhelming when it comes to our children's futures. New technologies seem to be arising almost every day, and with so many innovations, it creates unique professions which many of us wouldn't have dreamed to be necessary only a few years ago. Which to me is a good thing. Because with so much variety, my children can have the opportunity to pick a career that will fit their personalities and build upon their strengths. As you may imagine, this desire within me to provide my children with the resources they needed to thrive, led me to search out books that would be easy enough for them to understand while teaching them about various professions.

Only, I found that these books were few and far between. Even if I could find a book about a certain profession geared towards young readers, I found them sparse inside and limited to only certain careers that may not fit my children's abilities. This is when I came up with the idea to write my own children's books, teaching them about all the various careers in the modern world. After months of researching different professions and learning more than I ever expected, I quickly realised this was going to be a bigger project than I first anticipated. I dove into the histories of these professions, discovering links to the past, and why these professions were now so important.

Ultimately my goal was to offer my children options, to show them that there is no one set path for everyone. But in this, I stumbled upon something bigger. I wanted to share this with future generations. To share with all children and parents about these careers, to help spark curiosity, and to instil a passion for the future. Everyone has special talents and abilities, and I hope that this series will be able to offer clarity and inspiration to children around the world. Because at the end of the day, it's never too early to start dreaming and never too late to take action. With this, I hope you enjoy this series and that your young ones become the best versions of themselves as they can achieve.